CONTENTS

Masters of *land, sea,* and *sky,* birds have *conquered* **every corner** of the globe – from the **frozen wastes** of Antarctica to the **highest mountains** and *driest deserts*. If you look out of a window for a second or simply close your eyes, the animals you're most likely to see or hear first are **BIRDS**. The *secret* of their **success** is the ***ability to fly***. The first birds were feathery reptiles that took to the sky 150 million years ago. We may never know how they discovered the knack of *riding on air*.

Everything you need to know about
BIRDS

Penguin Random House

Editor Ishani Nandi
Art editor Nehal Verma
Project editor Sam Priddy
Senior editor Shatarupa Chaudhuri
Senior art editor Nishesh Batnagar
Managing editors Laura Gilbert,
Alka Thakur Hazarika
Managing art editors Diane Peyton Jones,
Romi Chakraborty
DTP designer Bimlesh Tiwary
CTS manager Balwant Singh
Pre-production Dragana Puvacic
Producer Srijana Gurung
Senior picture researcher Sumedha Chopra
Jacket designer Kartik Gera
Publisher Sarah Larter
Publishing director Sophie Mitchell
Art director Stuart Jackman
Consultant Derek Harvey

Previously published in 2009 in Canada, France,
Germany, and the Netherlands as *Swoop*.
This edition first published in Great Britain in 2016
by Dorling Kindersley Limited,
80 Strand, London WC2R 0RL.

Copyright © 2009, © 2016
Dorling Kindersley Limited, London
A Penguin Random House Company

2 4 6 8 10 9 7 5 3 1
001–265423–Feb/2016

A CIP catalogue record for this book
is available from the British Library.

ISBN 978-0-2412-2791-6

Printed and bound in China

A WORLD OF IDEAS:
SEE ALL THERE IS TO KNOW
www.dk.com

Perhaps they lived in trees and began *gliding* from branch to branch. Or perhaps they scampered along the ground, making the occasional **leap** into the air or **swooping** down a cliff. The **power of flight** gave birds the ultimate means of *escaping predators* and reaching new **habitats**. Today there are around **10,000** *different species* of bird ranging from bee-sized hummingbirds to flightless **GIANTS** and torpedo-shaped divers.

Welcome to the *wonderful world of birds.*

Birds have made a home on every continent and in almost every habitat, from frozen polar regions to dry deserts and open oceans.

Forest

The greatest variety of birds live in forests. Fruit, nuts, berries, seeds, insects, and other small animals are easy pickings for food. Twigs and leaves are ideal for nest-making, while tree trunks can make good solid homes for those that can find a handy hollow.

Grassland

Open pastures, grassy fields, prairies, or savannas… Grasslands of all types provide lush feeding grounds for seed-eating and insect-eating birds, such as this finch. In winter, pasture is used by grazing waterfowl such as geese and swans.

Polar

Warm feathers are a must when you live in polar regions. Most birds don't stay all year round – they migrate to warmer, drier land during the winter – but some remain all year, such as the Antarctic's Emperor Penguin.

Wetland

Freshwater wetlands such as lakes and rivers attract a huge variety of birds, from ducks to songbirds to pelicans. The water teems with fish, algae, and other food, while reeds can be the perfect bedding material.

Scrubland

Wild, open areas of scrubland – which occur where it is too wet for deserts but too dry for forests to grow – attract a huge variety of birds from nectar-eaters to birds of prey. While there is plenty of food, there are few trees, so some birds nest on the ground.

Desert

Deserts get less than 25 cm (10 in) of rainfall a year. Most birds avoid these dry regions, but some species can cope with droughts. Sandgrouse soak up water in their breast feathers and then fly back to their nest so the chicks can suck the feathers for a drink.

Mountain

The higher the altitude, the harder life is for birds. Large birds cover a wide area searching for food, while small birds peck for seeds and insects among the few plants. Perhaps the hardiest bird is the Red-billed Chough – it has been seen at the summit of Mount Everest.

Ocean

No bird can spend all its life at sea, but the Sooty Tern comes close, flying over tropical oceans for two to three months before coming to land to breed. The Ancient Murrelet, a member of the puffin family, even raises its chicks entirely at sea.

Coast

Birds have settled on almost every stretch of coastline in the world. Some birds come inland for food; others fly out to sea in their search for fresh fish. Long-billed seabirds probe for food in the coastal mud – but they might never actually see what it is they're eating!

Urban

It's thought that there are more birds in cities than there are people. Some species spread there naturally, but two of the most numerous – pigeons and starlings – were introduced by people. Many roost on rooftops and window ledges – the ideal substitutes for their natural habitat of cliffs.

THERE ARE MORE THAN 10,600 DIFFERENT SPECIES

Tinamous

Ostriches

Rheas

Cassowaries and Emus

Kiwis

Gamebirds

Waterfowl

Penguins

Loons

Albatrosses and Petrels

Grebes

Flamingos

Storks and Herons

Pelicans

Birds of prey

Birds are grouped in the class known as Aves.
This is the Latin word for bird, and gives us the
term "avian" when talking about something
being birdy. Birds are further classified into
204 families under 29 orders. The orders to the
left of the tree are said to be "primitive" – they
evolved first and have changed less over time
than the orders on the right. But all birds share
a common ancestry: dinosaurs.

More than **50%** of all known bird species are **passerines** (perching birds)

There is one common link that groups all 6,300 passerine species into one order...

Hang on! We can perch, but we're budgies, not passerines!

They are characterized by having **four long, flexible toes** – three pointing forwards and one backwards. All of the toes join the foot at the same level.

But you don't perch in the same way I do. Bet you can't do THIS!

Toes like these allow them to perch safely on tiny twigs, bendy stems, and thin telephone wires, even in strong winds. It's even safe to fall asleep on the perch, as **the toes instantly lock into position** when they land.

The word "passerine" comes from the Latin *passer*, which means sparrow — but not all passerines look like sparrows.

Just 6.5 cm (2½ in) long and weighing less than 5 gm (⅕ oz), the smallest passerine is the **Short-tailed Pygmy Tyrant.**

The largest passerine is the **Common Raven**. Some species of raven from colder regions can weigh up to 2 kg (4½ lbs) – 400 times heavier than the pygmy tyrant.

Many passerines are migratory. It was once thought that tiny Goldcrests hitched a ride on the backs of owls to cross the sea, but, in fact, they can make the journey by themselves.

Bird heaven
The Manu Biosphere Reserve in Peru is home to more than 1,000 species of bird, including seven species of macaw and 22 other types of parrot. That's more bird species than can be found in the whole of the USA and Canada combined.

Keep it green

Birds play an important part in maintaining the rainforest. Fruit eaters, such as parrots and toucans, spread tree seeds through their droppings. Hummingbirds help pollinate flowers when they visit them to drink nectar.

The AMAZON is home to 12 per cent

Emergent layer

The tops of trees are home to some of the biggest birds of the rainforest, such as eagles, hawks, toucans, and parrots.

Canopy

With its intertwined branches and vines, the canopy is an ideal habitat for smaller birds to build nests and hide from predators.

Understorey

Birds that feed on the forest floor make their nests here. Others come to feast on flowers and sweet nectar.

Tree trunks

The tall trunks of rainforest trees are ideal for woodpeckers and woodcreepers, which use their long bills to probe for insects under the bark.

Forest floor

This is the darkest part of the rainforest. The birds that live here are mainly dull in colour to match the fallen leaves all around them on the ground. They eat insects, reptiles, frogs, leaves, and fallen fruit.

The rainforest of the Amazon basin covers an area almost as big as Australia. Around 2,000 species of bird live in this region.

Amazon basin

South America

Australia

Harpy Eagle

Scarlet Macaw

Canary-winged Parakeet

Violaceous Trogon

Swallow-tailed Hummingbird

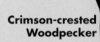

Band-tailed Manakin

Warbling Antbird

Crimson-crested Woodpecker

Long-billed Woodcreeper

Grey-winged Trumpeter

Sunbittern

of the world's BIRD species.

BIRD evolution

Fossils can teach us a lot about the origins of birds and how they evolved. But scientists disagree on exactly how they came to rule the skies. Most experts believe they are descendents of dinosaurs; others think they evolved separately. As more fossil evidence is found, we get a clearer picture of how they came to be.

4.5 billion to 418 million years ago (mya)

The Earth and oceans formed. The very first life forms lived under water because the surface was too hot and there was not enough oxygen in the atmosphere to support life on land.

354–290 mya

Tetrapods left the water to live on land. By the end of the Carboniferous period they had begun to lay eggs on land instead of in the water. This development is called the amniotic egg. Eggs began to have a protective shell to prevent the embryo (unborn animal) from drying out.

Ichthyostega

240 mya

A group of reptiles called ornithodirans appeared. These were the ancestors of dinosaurs, pterosaurs (flying reptiles), and birds.

Eoraptor

230 mya

Theropods, a type of dinosaur, appeared. Thought to be the ancestors of birds, they walked on two legs, had fingers and toes with claws, and a long neck.

Herrerasaurus

418–354 mya

Some fish began to walk on lobed fins, which developed into limbs. These early tetrapods (four-limbed animals) ventured into shallow waters and breathed oxygen from the improving atmosphere into their developing lungs. They became the first amphibians.

Tiktaalik

290–252 mya

The first reptiles flourished. Some lived in the water, but a group called archosaurs, or "ruling reptiles", evolved on land. They had scaly skin and beak-like mouths, some with pointed teeth. Many smaller reptiles began climbing trees.

Archosaur

Fossils suggest that feather-like structures began to appear on dinosaurs. Though initially disputed, today, most experts agree that some dinosaurs had feathers.

EARLY ERAS	DEVONIAN	CARBONIFEROUS	PERMIAN	TRIASSIC
up to 418 million years ago (mya)	418–354 mya	354–290 mya	290–252 mya	252–199.5 mya

Early amphibian   Tetrapod   Archosaur   Theropod dinosaur

4 billion years ago   2 billion years ago   **400** million years ago (mya)   **300**

The first pterosaurs took to the skies. They had membrane wings like those of bats, and a toothed beak on a bird-like skull. Pterosaurs did not evolve into birds.

220 mya

Dimorphodon

Caudipteryx fossils show that it had a mixture of dinosaur and bird features. It had a bird-like beak, feathers, and a short tail, but the teeth and bones of a dinosaur. It was unable to fly.

125 mya

Caudipteryx

Archaeopteryx appeared – classed as the first true bird. It had flight feathers, but its breastbone was too small to support flight muscles. It could probably only glide from branches rather than fly by flapping. It had a long, bony tail, claws on its wings, and a toothed bill.

150 mya

Archaeopteryx

120 mya

The magpie-sized Confucius bird perched in trees, ate plants, and was a strong flyer. It had a stubby tail with long feathers and a horny, toothless bill.

65 mya – A mass extinction event killed 95 per cent of all life on the planet, including the dinosaurs.

The differences between bird species were key to Darwin's **theory of evolution.**

Confuciusornis

A number of small theropods are believed to have been covered with a furry down of simple feathers, which they used for warmth rather than flight.

145 mya

Compsognathus

Hesperornis

The first seabirds evolved in the late Cretaceous period. *Hesperornis* was a huge, long-necked, flightless bird. It had large webbed feet and was a powerful swimmer.

60 mya

Many flightless birds survived extinction. They went on to become ratites, such as moas and elephant birds. They were eventually succeeded by the ostriches, emus, rheas, and kiwis seen today. The last moas and elephant birds were hunted to extinction by humans, dying out about 300 years ago. Some waterbirds also survived and these eventually gave rise to other species of modern birds.

Elephant bird

140 mya

Dromaeosaurs were feathered dinosaurs that shared similarities to birds, including three clawed fingers on each hand.

160 mya

A fossil of *Epidexipteryx* shows it had a set of showy tail feathers, probably used for display. There is no evidence it could fly.

Epidexipteryx

Velociraptor, a dromaeosaur

80 mya

Rise of the euornithes or "true birds". These had toothless, horny bills, and a four-chambered heart to help rapid muscle movement during flight. However, most died out during the great extinction event that killed the dinosaurs and pterosaurs at the end of the Cretaceous period.

Ichthyornis

A group of flightless "terror birds" dominated South America. Some stood more than 3 m (10 ft) tall and could run at 50 kph (30 mph).

60–2 mya

Titanis, the terror bird

JURASSIC	CRETACEOUS	TERTIARY
199.5–142 mya	142–65 mya	65 mya–present

Early bird

Feathered dinosaur

Terror bird

And finally...
Modern humans didn't show up on Earth until around 250,000 years ago. That means birds have existed 150 million years longer than us.

Rhea

200

100

NOW

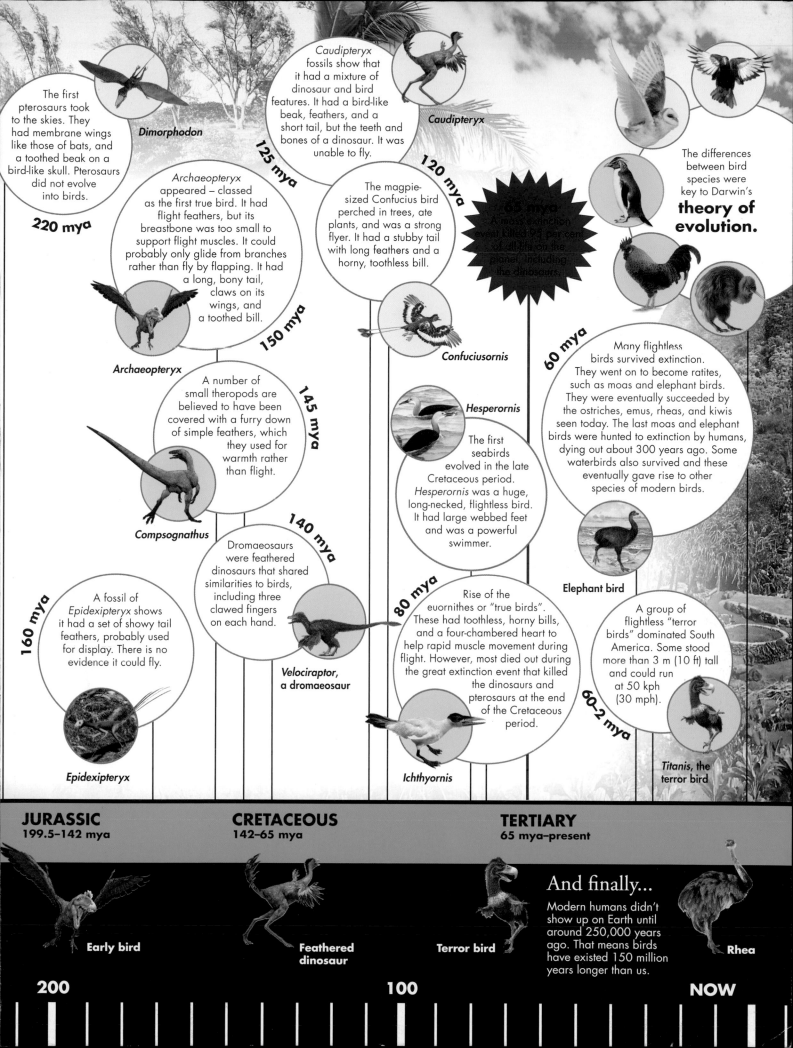

In 1969, a scientist called Dr John Ostrom compared *Archaeopteryx* (the first bird) to a theropod dinosaur. He discovered they shared 22 features. Later scientists have found around 100 similarities. Could this be proof that birds evolved from dinosaurs?

SPOT THE

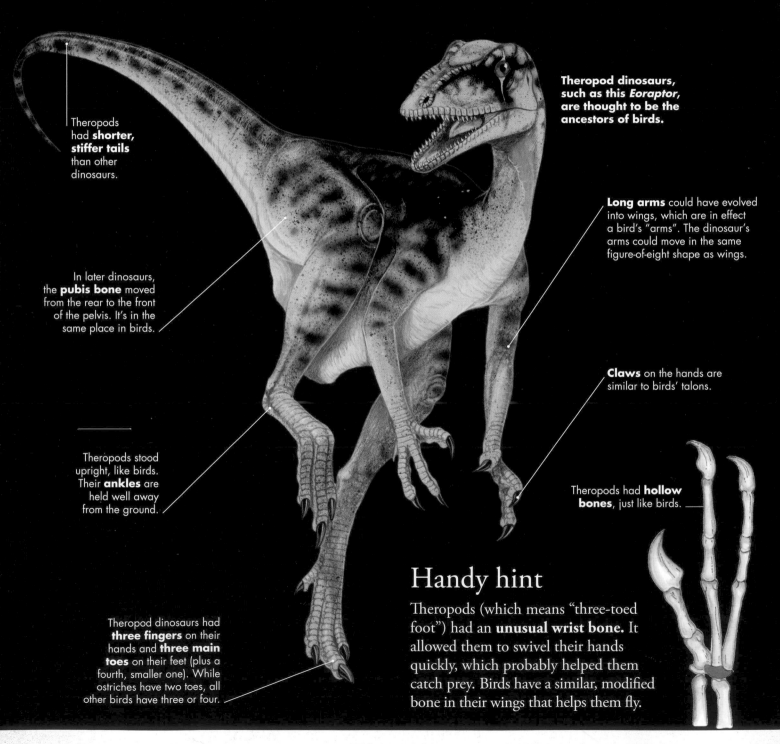

Theropods had **shorter, stiffer tails** than other dinosaurs.

Theropod dinosaurs, such as this *Eoraptor*, are thought to be the ancestors of birds.

Long arms could have evolved into wings, which are in effect a bird's "arms". The dinosaur's arms could move in the same figure-of-eight shape as wings.

In later dinosaurs, the **pubis bone** moved from the rear to the front of the pelvis. It's in the same place in birds.

Claws on the hands are similar to birds' talons.

Theropods stood upright, like birds. Their **ankles** are held well away from the ground.

Theropods had **hollow bones**, just like birds.

Theropod dinosaurs had **three fingers** on their hands and **three main toes** on their feet (plus a fourth, smaller one). While ostriches have two toes, all other birds have three or four.

Handy hint

Theropods (which means "three-toed foot") had an **unusual wrist bone.** It allowed them to swivel their hands quickly, which probably helped them catch prey. Birds have a similar, modified bone in their wings that helps them fly.

There are many similarities between an

DIFFERENCE

Large, air-filled cavities in the skull are common to birds and theropods.

Like theropods, birds have **huge eyes**.

Many animals have collarbones made up of separate bones. In birds, the bones have fused (joined) together to make the wishbone. Theropods had a similar **fused collarbone**.

It's easy to compare an ostrich's long, S-shaped neck to that of an *Eoraptor*. Unlike other animals, birds have **lots of neck bones**.

All birds have **feathers**, and some recently discovered fossil evidence suggests that some dinosaurs did, too.

A bird's **shoulderblade** is the same shape as a theropod's.

The **bones of a bird's toes** are long, like in a theropod's foot.

Both birds and dinosaurs have **feet** that are positioned directly underneath their bodies.

The **ankle joint** is like a hinge – it moves backwards and forwards.

Dinosaur DNA?

Some people claim that ostriches are so similar to dinosaurs, we could use their eggs to bring dinosaurs back to life. But that's impossible – to create a dinosaur, you need a complete string of DNA (chemical instructions that tell a body how to grow), and not enough dinosaur DNA exists.

Eoraptor and an ostrich. Could it be coincidence?

17

Built for flight

Almost everything about a bird's anatomy is designed for flight.

With lightweight skeletons, streamlined bodies, wings, and feathers, birds have evolved to be masters of the air.

Hollow bones

If you want to fly, it helps to be as light as possible. Human bones are heavy, but bird bones have a structure like honeycomb. This makes the bones light yet strong enough for flight. The skeleton of a bird that can fly weighs less than 10 per cent of its body weight.

Skeleton

Birds have fewer bones than mammals. Many have fused together, which makes the skeleton more rigid. However, they have more neck bones than mammals do. This allows them to twist and turn the head to reach every part of their body. The skull is usually paper-thin but very strong.

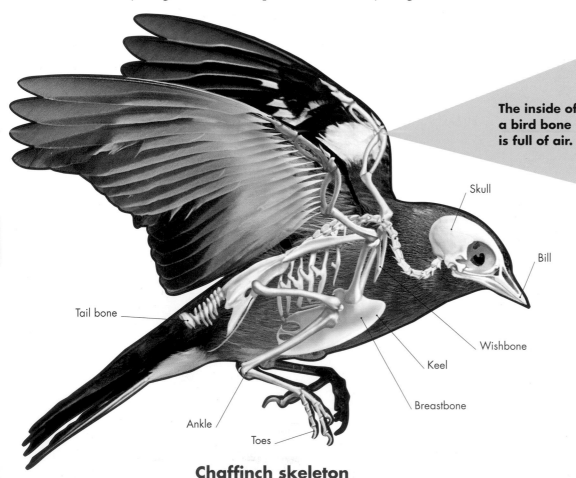

The inside of a bird bone is full of air.

Skull

Bill

Wishbone

Keel

Breastbone

Tail bone

Ankle

Toes

Chaffinch skeleton

Keel

The largest single bone in the bird's body is the breastbone, which has a keel that sticks out at right angles. Powerful flight muscles are attached to the keel. Above the keel is the wishbone, which acts like a spring when a bird flaps its wings.

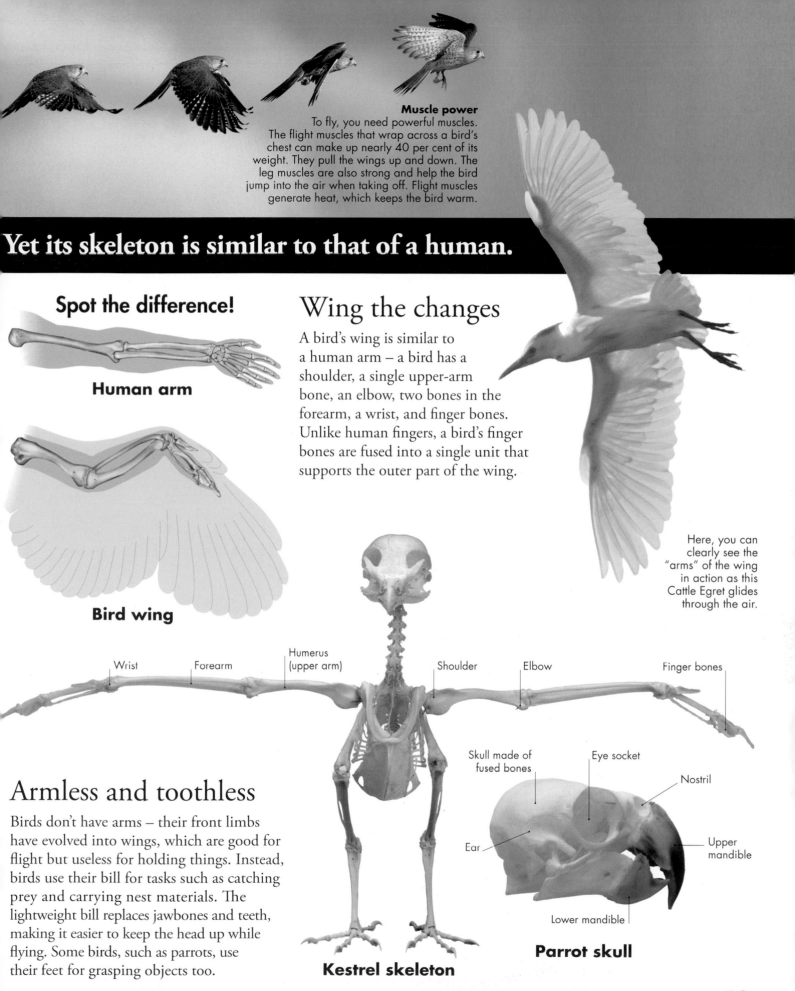

Muscle power
To fly, you need powerful muscles. The flight muscles that wrap across a bird's chest can make up nearly 40 per cent of its weight. They pull the wings up and down. The leg muscles are also strong and help the bird jump into the air when taking off. Flight muscles generate heat, which keeps the bird warm.

Yet its skeleton is similar to that of a human.

Spot the difference!

Human arm

Bird wing

Wing the changes

A bird's wing is similar to a human arm – a bird has a shoulder, a single upper-arm bone, an elbow, two bones in the forearm, a wrist, and finger bones. Unlike human fingers, a bird's finger bones are fused into a single unit that supports the outer part of the wing.

Here, you can clearly see the "arms" of the wing in action as this Cattle Egret glides through the air.

Wrist   Forearm   Humerus (upper arm)   Shoulder   Elbow   Finger bones

Armless and toothless

Birds don't have arms – their front limbs have evolved into wings, which are good for flight but useless for holding things. Instead, birds use their bill for tasks such as catching prey and carrying nest materials. The lightweight bill replaces jawbones and teeth, making it easier to keep the head up while flying. Some birds, such as parrots, use their feet for grasping objects too.

Skull made of fused bones   Eye socket   Nostril   Ear   Upper mandible   Lower mandible

Parrot skull

Kestrel skeleton

These feet were made for...

hunting

Owls rely on the element of surprise to catch prey. Thick feathers that reach all the way down to the ends of their wings help muffle sound so they can swoop silently down onto the unsuspecting animal. Then, with talons bared, the owl grabs the prey and carries it back to its roost.

perching

Passerines, or perching birds, have flexible feet that can grip on to the thinnest perch – even telephone wires. The toes lock into place when the bird settles, so the grip remains strong when the bird is asleep. Small songbirds can even hang upside-down by one leg.

killing

Birds of prey, such as this Red-tailed Hawk, are the only birds that use their feet (rather than their bill) to kill prey. A hawk will fly in behind its prey, its feet pointing forwards and talons outstretched for the kill. The rear talon is usually the strongest, and often delivers the fatal stab.

walking on water

In their search for food, jacanas walk across lily leaves that float on the surface of pools. Their long toes help spread the weight of the bird (which isn't very heavy anyway) so they won't sink. From a distance it can look like the bird is walking on water.

running

Most birds have four toes, but ostriches are unique in that they have just two. Smaller feet mean there is less of a surface to come in contact with the ground. This reduces friction when running, allowing the ostrich to reach speeds of up to 72 kph (45 mph).

paddling

Swimming is so much easier with flippers to push against the water. Many waterbirds, such as this duck, have flaps of skin connecting their three forward-facing toes. A duckling fleeing danger can swim so fast, it almost runs on the surface of the water.

mating

Why do Blue-footed Boobies have blue feet? So they look different from Red-footed Boobies! Females need to tell the species apart so they know which males they can mate with. Helpfully, the males perform a courtship dance to show off their feet.

Sight

You **know** it makes **sense**

Birds have all the same senses as humans, but rely most on sight and hearing. These help them find food, attract mates, spot predators, and fly with great accuracy.

Some, but not all, birds have a good sense of smell. Others have a touch-sensitive bill or whiskers that they use to detect worms in soil or shellfish in mud. Taste is the least developed sense, but it is good enough to help them avoid poisonous foods.

I'm keeping an eye on you. The other one's on that cat...

Starlings, like most birds, have excellent vision. Their eyes are very large compared to the rest of their body, and can move independently to see what's happening on either side of the bird.

Predators, such as hawks, can see further than other birds. They can spot a mouse on the ground 1,600 m (5,250 ft) below them. Vultures can spot carcasses from more than twice that distance.

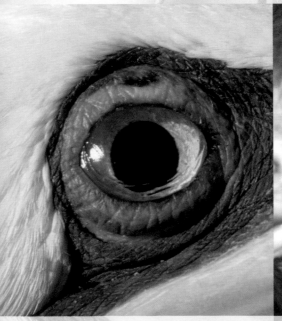

Gannets, boobies, and other diving birds have forward-facing eyes. They can spot fish from high above the sea and calculate how far a fish will move as they plunge into the water after it.

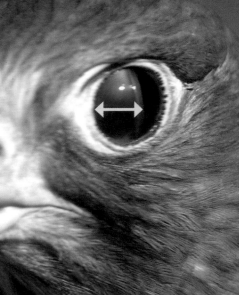

Birds have a transparent third eyelid that slides horizontally across the eyeball to clean it. It also acts like a windshield to protect the eye when flying or diving underwater.

Smell

Feather tufts (not ears)

The ears are at the side of the owl's head

Mmm... smells good. Think it's going to be fish for supper.

Owls have extremely good hearing. Their bowl-shaped faces act like a radar dish, focusing sound waves towards the ears. Some species hunt entirely by sound, listening for the slightest movement of an animal on the ground.

Petrels have an exceptional sense of smell. Like many seabirds, they can smell fish oils floating on the surface of the sea after sharks or dolphins attack schools of prey many miles away. They fly in and pick up the leftovers.

Is it just me, or is there an echo in here... here... here?

Come out, little worm – I know you're down there!

Oilbirds are like bats – they use echolocation to find their way in and out of the dark caves in which they roost. They call and listen for an echo to come back. They can tell where the cave roof and walls are by how quickly the sound returns.

Kiwis are unique in having their nostrils at the end of their bills. This helps them sniff out insects and earthworms in the undergrowth, which is useful since kiwis are nocturnal and have poor eyesight.

Digestive

Stomach

A bird's stomach is split into two parts. The first is the glandular stomach, where digestive acids are released. Birds of prey have large glandular stomachs – the Bearded Vulture (also known as the Lammergeier) has such powerful stomach acid that it can digest bones as thick as a person's wrist.

Gizzard

Birds have no teeth (a weight-saving feature), so they can't chew food before swallowing. Instead, muscles in the second stomach compartment, called the gizzard, mash the food. Seed-eating birds often swallow small stones and sand along with their food. These stay in the gizzard, helping to grind the food.

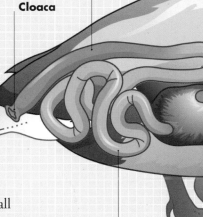

Oesophagus

Glandular stomach

Large intestine

Cloaca

Bill

Crop

Gizzard

Small intestine

Big mouth!

A bird can open its bill surprisingly wide to swallow food – many seabirds often guzzle down whole fish. The prize for the biggest bill goes to the Dalmatian Pelican. Its bill grows to 47 cm (18½ in) long, and the stretchy pouch can hold up to 13 litres (3 gallons) of water.

Crop

Many birds have a crop, or food store, in their chest. This enables them to eat fast and store food temporarily until they can find a safe place to sit and digest it properly. A bird can also regurgitate food from its crop to feed its chicks or to shed weight quickly if it needs to flee from danger.

The digestive system needs to work fast to deal with most birds' large intake of food.

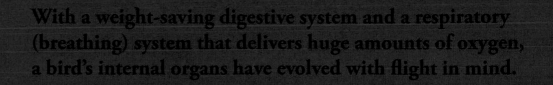

With a weight-saving digestive system and a respiratory (breathing) system that delivers huge amounts of oxygen, a bird's internal organs have evolved with flight in mind.

Respiratory

Breathe like a bird

When we breathe, air flows in and out of our lungs, which are never fully empty – there's always some stale air left. In birds, air flows into air sacs that are connected to the lungs. These air sacs hold freshly inhaled air, which flows into the lungs after stale air is released. This provides the bird a constant flow of fresh oxygen.

Hearts aflutter

The average human heart beats 70–75 times a minute, but birds have a heart rate of 400–600 beats per minute – and that's while they're resting! When flying, the rate can increase to 1,000 beats per minute. Small hummingbirds have an even faster maximum heart rate – up to 1,300 beats per minute – that's more than 21 every second.

Sackloads of air

As well as having lungs, most birds have nine air sacs. In diving birds, the sacs aren't very developed – the trapped air would make the bird float rather than sink. But in some land-based birds, the sacs reach from the throat to the toes.

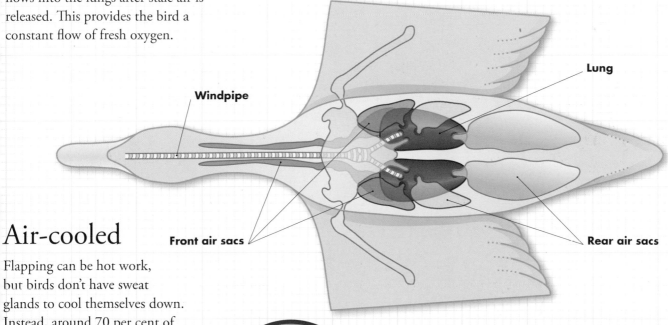

Windpipe

Lung

Front air sacs

Rear air sacs

Air-cooled

Flapping can be hot work, but birds don't have sweat glands to cool themselves down. Instead, around 70 per cent of the air they breathe is used for cooling. Some migratory birds that fly cruise high in the sky where the air is cooler, to stop them from overheating on long-distance journeys.

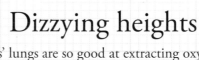

Dizzying heights

Birds' lungs are so good at extracting oxygen that they can breathe even at very high altitudes where the thin air would be lethal to humans. Birds have no problems flying at 10,000 m (6 miles) above sea level, but we would be unconscious that high up.

Air also flows into the bird's hollow bones. It's a complex system, but very efficient.

25

Feathers *galore*

The one feature that sets birds apart from all other animals isn't their bills, or wings, or that they lay eggs – there are other animals that have or do these things too. What makes birds unique is that they have feathers.

Contour feathers and down feathers cover the bird's body, providing warmth and waterproofing.

Flexible flight
Light, strong, and flexible, a bird's wing is the perfect design for flight. And light, strong, and flexible feathers are a vital part of that design.

Red-tailed Hawk

Graceful gliders
Red-tailed Hawks typically have broad, rounded wings that flap in slow, deliberate beats to gain height. Once high enough, they prefer gliding to conserve energy.

Turn left now
Spreading out the primary flight feathers helps a bird steer during flight. The gaps between the feathers also reduce turbulence for a smoother ride.

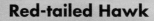

Birds are the only animals...

A weighty issue
There are fewer feathers on the wings than on the body. Despite individual feathers being very light, a bird's plumage (all its feathers) weighs more than its skeleton!

Covert feathers overlap the base of the flight feathers, making a smooth, streamlined covering.

The **alula feathers** cover the bird's "thumb". The alula can be raised to reduce turbulence, just like the flaps on an aeroplane's wing.

Secondary flight feathers give the wing a curved shape for lift.

Primary flight feathers are attached to the bird's "hand". They provide power and manoeuvrability for flight. A bird can still fly with the odd feather missing – perhaps with even as many as half of its secondaries gone. But it could not fly with half of its primaries missing – they really are essential.

Most birds have 12 **tail feathers**, which are used for braking, steering, and balance. Above them, on the base of the tail, are covert feathers.

A flurry of feathers

There are three main types of feather: flight, down, and contour (or body). Each has its own different shape and function. Flight feathers cover the bird's wings and are essential for keeping it airborne. Down feathers, which lie next to the bird's skin underneath the contour feathers, keep the bird warm. Contour feathers protect the bird's body and have a variety of functions from waterproofing to camouflage. They also include the tail feathers, which may be used in flight, for balance, or for display.

... t at have feat ers.

Look closer...

> Feathers are made from keratin – the same substance rhino horns, fish scales, and human fingernails are made of.

There's more to a feather than meets the eye. What appears to be a single, flat vane is actually made up of hundreds of barbs joined together with thousands of barbules.

Light fantastic
Some birds have feathers that look almost metallic. The way the feathers reflect light is known as iridescence.

Outer vane

Bubbles are also iridescent

A feather's backbone
The shaft of a feather is a hollow tube riddled with air pockets to keep it lightweight.

Shaft

Velcro®

Barb

Barbule

Stuck on you
Minuscule barbules act just like Velcro®, hooking the barbs together to make a smooth, even surface. This helps a bird fly efficiently.

28

Watch me grOW

Feathers grow out of follicles in the skin, a bit like hair on humans. As the feather gets longer, it develops barbs and barbules. Unlike human hair, feathers stop growing when they reach full-size.

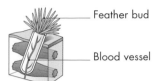

Feather bud

Blood vessel

Skin

Muscle to raise or lower feather

Shaft

Inner vane

Special FEATHERS

Bristles
Short, bristle-like feathers around a frogmouth's bill trap insects and sweep the meal into its open mouth.

Eyelashes
Long feathers over an ostrich's eyes act like eyelashes, keeping dirt and dust away from the eyeballs.

Noisemakers
Stiff feathers in a snipe's tail make a loud drumming sound as the bird performs a diving flight during courtship.

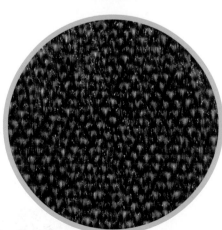

Scales
Penguin feathers are short and tough. They are packed together tightly like fish scales.

flight

If you've ever watched a bird fly overhead and wondered how it stays up in the air, you're not alone. For centuries, people have envied birds and tried to copy them by building fantastic flying machines. But for birds, flight is simply second nature.

HOW DOES A BIRD FLY?
It takes a lot of effort to fly. Birds have to produce two forces – lift and thrust – to gain height and keep moving forwards. But for each of these forces, there is another force holding them back. These are called drag and gravity. Gravity is what pulls all objects towards the Earth's surface. Drag is caused by air pushing against the bird's wings and body. Too much drag would eventually cause the bird to slow down and it wouldn't have enough speed to fly.

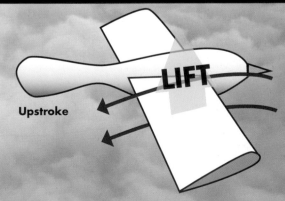

LIFT
... is produced by the stream of air flowing over the wings.

DRAG
... reduces the bird's speed.

THRUST
... is generated by flapping the wings, and pushes the bird forwards.

GRAVITY
... pulls all things downwards towards the Earth.

Feathers + wings + a light, air-filled skeleton = flight

Downstroke

LIFT

Aerofoil

KEEPING UP
If you could look at a cross-section of a bird's wing you would see that its upper surface is curved like that of an aeroplane. This curved shape is called an aerofoil. Air moves over the upper surface of the wing faster than the lower surface, producing lift. The faster the flow of air, the greater the lift. If there is enough lift to overcome gravity, the bird will rise.

Upstroke

LIFT

FLAPPING FLIGHT
Birds flap their wings in an up-and-down motion. The bird instinctively angles the wing for each upstroke and downstroke. On a downstroke the bird dips the front of the wing towards the ground, which increases its speed and lift. It raises the front of the wing for an upstroke. This produces lift on the inner part of the wing, but less than on a downstroke. This is why birds appear to bob up and down when they fly.

UP, UP, UP... and away!

Greater Flamingo

Take-off and landing are the trickiest parts of bird flight. It's all a question of speed.

Little birds have it easy – they just lift their wings, jump, and flap a few strokes and they're airborne. It's much harder if you're a big bird – you have to build up enough speed to lift your weight off the ground. First you lean into the wind and start running. Then you beat your wings in time with each step, getting faster and faster until you reach the critical airspeed. Then, stretch out your wings and you're off into the wide blue sky.

Takeoff

SOARING AND GLIDING

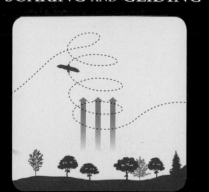

Flapping flight uses a lot of energy, so many large birds take advantage of opportunities to soar or glide. Gliding involves holding the wings out and tipping the body forwards to gain speed. Soaring makes use of thermals (warm currents of air rising from the ground). Seeking out these thermals, birds spiral round in them to gain height.

Taking off is easier for little birds.

Jump start
Small birds gain lift by jumping, then twisting their wings up and forwards on the downstroke, which pulls the bird up.

Great Tit

Braking hard
When they want to land, they drop their speed until they are just about to stop. With wings spread and tail down, they come to an abrupt halt.

Whooper Swan

Landing

Landing is harder than takeoff. The bird gradually slows its wingbeats and angles its wings so they act like a parachute. As the bird nears the ground, it spreads its tail and angles it downwards.

Feet first
Waterbirds use their webbed feet when they land on water. They stick them out and use them like water skis to slow themselves down.

Leonardo da Vinci *– artist,*

Leonardo was fascinated by the way birds flew. Could a man ever fly like a bird? He was determined to find out. He examined their wing structures and watched how birds moved them in flight. These studies inspired him to design a multitude of flying machines such as the man-powered "ornithopter" shown here.

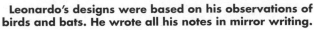

Model of Leonardo's ornithopter

Leonardo da Vinci (1452–1519)

Leonardo da Vinci was one of the most remarkable men of his time. He was not only a great artist, but also studied science, mathematics, anatomy, and engineering. He invented hundreds of machines, including cannons, siege engines, pumps, and musical instruments.

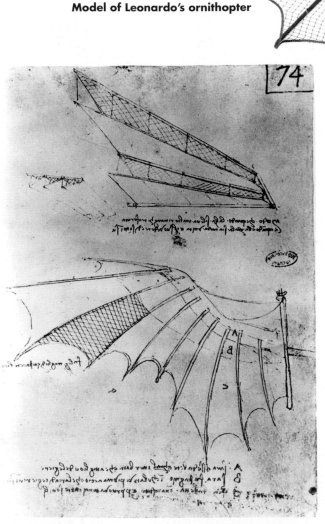

Leonardo's designs were based on his observations of birds and bats. He wrote all his notes in mirror writing.

Leonardo designed aeroplanes, gliders, and helicopters...

inventor... and PILOT?

Did it ever get off the ground?

Legend has it that one of Leonardo's students tried out one of his flying machines on Mount Ceceri, but crashed and broke a leg. A man could never generate enough power to fly such a heavy machine. Leonardo was also mistaken in thinking that birds flew by beating their wings downwards and backwards. What actually happens is that the wing feathers provide thrust on the downstroke, while the inner wing gives lift.

Harness

Ropes pull wings to make them flap.

The pilot pedals to flap the wings and steers with his hands.

Leonardo's glider

Of all Leonardo's flying machines, it was his last design for a glider, drawn less than 10 years before his death, that had the greatest potential for flight. In his description Leonardo says: "... this [man] will move on the right side if he bends the right arm and extends the left arm; and he will then move from right to left by changing the position of the arms."

One of Leonardo's designs had a ladder and undercarriage that could be pulled up after takeoff.

... 400 years before the first powered aircraft flight.

A year in the life of a GLOBETROTTER

Arctic Terns travel around the world on their extraordinary migrations between the edge of the Antarctic pack-ice and the Arctic circle. Some of them experience two polar summers in a year and see more daylight than any other animal on the Earth.

ARCTIC

20,000 km (12,500 miles) each way.

The journey from pole to pole is around

ANTARCTIC

Global satnav
It's amazing how a bird can find its way around our huge planet while migrating. Most birds navigate by sight, looking out for familiar landmarks and watching the movement of the Sun and stars. Birds also recognize sounds and smells, but perhaps most importantly, they have an in-built magnetic compass that picks up the Earth's magnetic field.

The Arctic Tern **MIGRATES FARTHER** in the course of its life than any other species of bird.

An individual breeding in the far north might clock up to **50,000 km (31,000 miles) ANNUALLY**, including feeding trips.

An Arctic Tern that survives into its mid-20s is likely to have flown approximately 765,000 km (475,000 miles) – the same distance as from **THE EARTH TO THE MOON AND BACK.**

By the end of its lifetime, an Arctic Tern could have travelled...

An Arctic Tern's home in the northern hemisphere may be as far north as the High Arctic or as far south as the UK or Hudson Bay, Canada. Those that live farther north fly the farthest, but those on the southern edge get home first! After their winter break, the first birds home are ready to breed by early May. More northerly birds will be home by June.

Map position **1**

Early May

The first birds arrive back to their nesting grounds and start looking for a mate.

June–July

Colonies are fiercely defended at the height of the breeding season.

Why fly so far?
Because it's worth it! There is plenty of food for the terns in the far north during summer but not in winter, whereas there is abundant food near the Antarctic in the southern summer but not very much in the southern winter. By migrating, the terns get to enjoy two food-filled summers every year! Also, the Sun barely sets in the Arctic midsummer, so there is lots of sunlight for breeding.

Arctic Terns are the only birds that regularly appear on all seven continents.

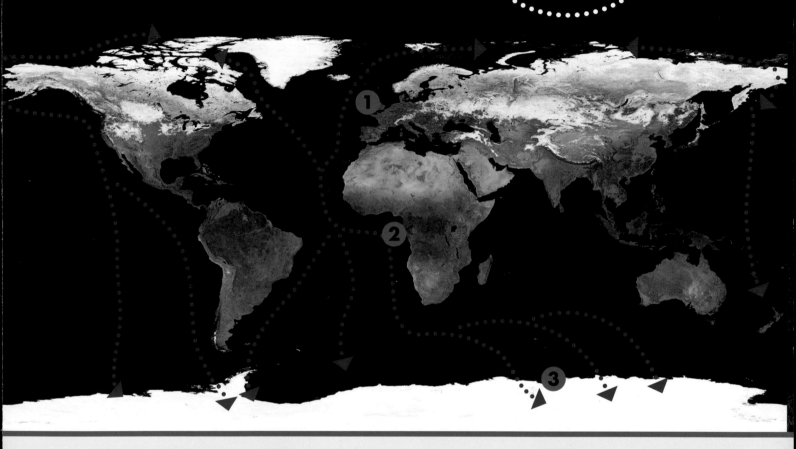

... more than **2.4 million km (1.5 million miles).**

Late July–August

In little over 60 days, the terns have formed pairs, built territories, and raised their young.

Map position 2 September–October

Chicks and adults migrate south. They prefer to fly near coasts, so it's not the quickest trip.

Map position 3 Mid-November

Krill are shrimp-like animals.

Reaching the pack-ice zone, the terns survive by eating krill.

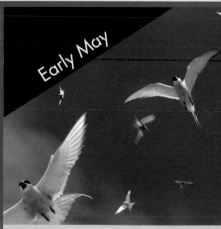

Early May

The terns begin migrating back to the nesting grounds where they hatched.

"As aviators, we have a love for the creatures that taught us the art of flying."

LEADING

May–June

Because Whooping Crane chicks are raised in captivity, volunteers must teach them everything about being a crane. As soon as the chicks hatch, they are cared for by people dressed up in crane costumes, who act as stand-in parents. As one volunteer said, "Just like real parents, we teach many things to our young birds and that often includes what to eat. We show them berries, grasshoppers, and corn. We get some crab and show them how to break the shell. It doesn't take long before they catch on."

The Whooping Crane of North America is a critically endangered species. Since 2001, an organization called Operation Migration has

"Training a Whooping Crane is really no different to training a dog… Whether asking a dog to sit and giving it a doggie biscuit, or getting a crane to follow a very noisy, very yellow machine by giving it mealworms or grapes, it is really all the same."

June–August

The chicks, aged less than a week old, are introduced to an ultralight glider. First they are trained to follow it along the ground. By August, when the chicks can fly, they are so used to the glider that they happily follow it into the air.

THE WAY

helped these rare birds to spread their wings. They hand-raise crane chicks through every stage of their life until they can fend for themselves. This is how they do it.

CRITICALLY ENDANGERED

Migration time!

The 2008 migration took 88 days in all, with 23 flying days. There were 23 stops on the way for the birds to rest and eat.

Wisconsin

Florida

October–December

As winter approaches, the cranes have to be taught the route from the sanctuary in Wisconsin to their wintering grounds in Florida. The 2,068 km (1,285 miles) journey crosses seven states and takes several months.

"What a thrill it was to see these nearly grown cranes flying free; completely free, with no handler calling them back, no ultralight leading them on, just going wherever the wind and their will led them."

March

After spending three months in Florida being cared for by volunteers, spring arrives and the cranes get itchy feet. They eat more, fly more, and begin to get ready for the long journey north – on their own.

I wish
I could *fly*...
but
I can't

• **Some flightless birds, such as ratites, don't have a keel on their breastbone. In flying birds, the flight muscles attach to the keel.**

Birds fly, don't they? Not all of them! More than 50 species stay on the ground (or on lakes, or in the sea) and never take to the skies. The most well known are the ratites – ostriches, emus, cassowaries, rheas, and kiwis. Their ancestors probably could fly, but over time they gradually lost the ability. Often, this was because they lived in places where there were no predators. If you don't need to fly, you don't need to waste energy powering wings.

You can't catch me

Ostriches are the biggest birds in the world. Not many predators take them on, as an ostrich can outrun most of them with its top speed of 72 kph (45 mph). While most flightless birds have small wings that are little more than stumps, ostriches have a wingspan of around 2 m (6½ ft). They don't use their wings for flying but for balance while they're running and for courtship displays.

Caution
Ostriches crossing!

- They have solid bones instead of the light spongy bones of birds that can fly.

- Most flightless birds have very short tails, or none at all.

- Their wing feathers are small or fluffy, so useless for flight. However, they have more feathers than flying birds.

Bird or hedgehog?

In some ways, kiwis are more like mammals than birds. These nocturnal birds (found in New Zealand) have tiny, barely visible wings; their long, thin feathers look like hair; and they have whiskers to detect insects in the undergrowth. Uniquely for a bird, their nostrils are at the end of their bill so they can snuffle for worms, just like hedgehogs do. Real hedgehogs, which were brought to New Zealand by humans, are a threat to kiwis as they like eating kiwi eggs.

Jumping parrot

Not all flightless birds are ratites – Kakapos are flightless parrots. They are the heaviest parrots in the world and one of only a few parrot types that are active at night. They are excellent climbers and can leap down from the tops of trees by spreading their wings and jumping from branch to branch. Kakapos are native to New Zealand, but just 124 remain as they are under threat from introduced predators.

Full steam ahead

Not to be confused with the Flying Steamer-Duck, which can fly but prefers not to, the Flightless Steamer-Duck has an alternative mode of transport – it imitates a ship! It's a big duck, but has small wings, which it moves in a circular motion through the water to propel itself just like a paddle steamship. Steamer ducks live in the Falkland Islands and around the coast of South America.

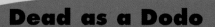

Dead as a Dodo

The main problem with having no wings is that you become an easy target for introduced predators – and people. Many flightless birds, such as moas and elephant birds, have become extinct or are on the verge of extinction, but no animal is more famously dead than the Dodo. This 1-m- (3-ft-) tall relative of the pigeon lived on Mauritius. Having never seen humans, Dodos were completely unafraid of them and became sitting targets for hunters. From their discovery in 1581, it took only 100 years for the Dodo to be wiped out and take its place in history.

Female Satin Bowerbird

True blue
baby, I love you

The rainforests of eastern Australia are a building site... for Satin Bowerbirds. The males build bowers (shady enclosures made of leaves and twigs) to attract females, then perform a courtship dance in front of them to tempt the female inside.

1 Bowerbird the Builder at your service, making walls out of sticks and stalks. I'll even line them with a paste of leaves.

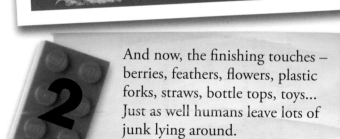

2 And now, the finishing touches — berries, feathers, flowers, plastic forks, straws, bottle tops, toys... Just as well humans leave lots of junk lying around.

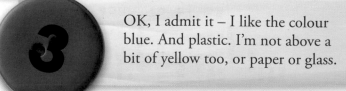

3 OK, I admit it — I like the colour blue. And plastic. I'm not above a bit of yellow too, or paper or glass.

This type of bower (called an "avenue") can be more than 1.5 m (5 ft) high.

4 It's worked! Someone's come! OK dear, you stay at the back and I'll do my dance for you out here. When you're ready, we'll both step inside... and later you can leave and build your own nest to lay your eggs in.

Love me,
Love my bower,
Can I tempt you inside
With a dance or
a flower?

Male Satin Bowerbird

What's inside an egg?

Eggs are amazing. They are structurally strong, and contain everything needed to grow a baby bird. If you carefully open a hen's egg, this is what you'll see.

Yolk
The yolk is the main source of nutrients for the growing bird. It contains protein, fat, minerals, and vitamins. The yellowness of the yolk depends on the type of bird and what it has been feeding on. The yolk is surrounded by a clear protective membrane.

Inner and outer membranes
Lining the shell and surrounding the albumen are two tough membranes that stop bacteria getting in. A layer of air between them cushions the liquid contents of the egg against the shell. As a warm, new-laid egg cools, an air cell forms at the blunt end of the egg, which grows bigger as the egg develops.

Albumen
Crack an egg and a transparent jelly falls out. This is called albumen, from the Latin word for "white", because this is the colour it turns if you cook it.

Chalaza
Sometimes you can see a twisted strand on each side of the yolk. This is called a chalaza. It connects the yolk to the inner membrane and holds the yolk steady in the middle of the egg.

Shell
Eggshells are made of calcium carbonate, which is the same mineral that makes up snail shells, sea shells, and chalk. Although eggshells look solid, they are covered in thousands of tiny holes that let air and moisture in and out. Most of these holes are at the blunt end of the egg. As the chick grows, it uses some of the calcium in the shell to make its bones.

Hen's egg

Air cell

Yolk membrane

SO, WHERE DO BABY BIRDS COME FROM? After birds have mated, the female lays an egg that contains an embryo, which develops into a chick. This is what happens after the egg is laid.

Day 4
The embryo has already grown a head, tail, and toes.

Day 10
All the limbs are growing and the internal organs are in place. The bill is visible.

Day 16
Feathers begin to appear on the body and scales on the legs. The bones and bill harden.

Day 20
The chick now breathes through its lungs. It points its head towards the air cell.

Day 21
Using the egg tooth on its bill, the chick breaks out. Happy birthday!

Top layers

egg facts

WANDERING ALBATROSS
These birds are almost a decade old before they start breeding and lay only one egg every two years. However, as they usually live to be at least 50 years, they can lay 20 eggs in a lifetime.

GOLDEN EAGLE
Eagles usually lay two eggs every year but fail to breed if weather conditions and food supplies are not right.

BLUE TIT
Tiny as these birds are, they can lay as many as 10–14 eggs in one clutch.

Cracking stuff

Why don't eggs break when a bird sits on them? Well, it's all down to their shape. Dome shapes are very strong, and the more curved they are, the more pressure they can resist. So, if you squeeze the pointed ends of an egg between your palms, it won't break. Squeeze it in the middle and you'll get egg on your face.

It's easier to crack an egg in the middle...

... than at an end.

STRONG   weak

NORTHERN BOBWHITE
Clutches vary between 6 and 28 eggs a year, though females will sometimes lay extra eggs in another bobwhite's nest.

There are machines that can crack and separate 108,000 eggs an hour. That's 30 a second!

If you cook an egg, the protein molecules in the yolk and albumen change shape. This is what makes them go hard and the albumen change colour.

DOMESTIC CHICKEN
Nothing can beat an ordinary chicken when it comes to laying eggs. The number of eggs chickens lay varies between different breeds, but some leghorns can lay as many as 300 a year. Left to their own devices, chickens would lay a clutch and then hatch them. But since most domestic chickens have been bred to lay infertile eggs (eggs that won't develop into a chick), this is unlikely to happen. Those that are kept on a farm lay about one egg a day, but because the egg is taken away, they lay another one. Chickens will only lay if they get the right amount of daylight, and usually produce one egg every 28 hours.

Some birds take only a few seconds to lay an egg. However, Canada Geese can take an hour to lay a single egg.

Birds usually lay their eggs in the morning. This is because eggshells form more easily when the bird is at roost.

A Nest is NOT a bird's home...

Birds don't build nests as a place to sleep or eat. They build them as a nursery to keep their eggs and chicks safe from predators. There are different types of nest, made out of whatever materials the birds have around them.

Common cups

Cups are the most common nest shape. Most passerines (perching birds) build these basic bowls. Sticks and twigs often form the main nest, but some birds, such as swallows, build their cups from mud or even saliva. Moss, animal fur, and feathers may be used to line the nest to keep the eggs warm.

... but it's a safe place to lay eggs and raise chicks.

Cavity nests are homely holes.

Mounds of mud are the only alternative in plant-free areas.

Sphere nests, made from woven grass, have a small opening for the parent to fly in and out.

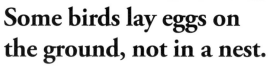

Some birds lay eggs on the ground, not in a nest.

Platform nests are flat – and huge!

Puffins use their feet to dig out **burrows**, which can be 1 m (3 ft) deep.

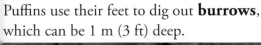

Spiderweb silk ties this nest together – and onto a leaf.

Who needs a nest when dad's feet are safe and warm?

Lady
in the
tower

Many birds nest in hollow trees, but none goes to the lengths of the hornbill to protect its offspring. After finding a large hole high in a tree, the female hornbill walls herself in, lays an egg, and sits there until her chick is ready to fly.

All holed up

Hornbills move into holes that have already been excavated by another bird, such as a woodpecker. Squeezing through an entrance barely big enough, the female cleans out the hole and lines it with new nesting material. When she is ready to lay an egg, she and her mate close up the hole using her droppings, which they paste around the entrance with their bills. She is almost entirely sealed in – the only gap is a thin slit wide enough for the tip of her bill to poke through.

Housekeeping

While she is incubating her egg, the female moults her flight feathers, and sometimes her tail feathers too. To keep the nest clean, she twists around and blasts her droppings out of the hole. The chick learns to do this when it hatches.

Alone together

It takes between one and two months for the chick to hatch. During that time, the female is fed by her mate, who brings her fruit, and occasionally, small animals. Once the chick is hatched, the female stays with it for about a month, then breaks out to help the male find food. Sometimes, the chick walls the hole back up again and stays there for a few more weeks. It eventually leaves the nest fully fledged (able to fly).

Success!

Despite this strange start in life, hornbills have a good success rate. Sealing the nest in a hole high up in a tree protects the egg and growing chick from most predators, including tree snakes. Although most species of hornbill raise only one chick, more than **75 per cent** of chicks make it to fledging.

Where's my mum?

Match the parent to the chick

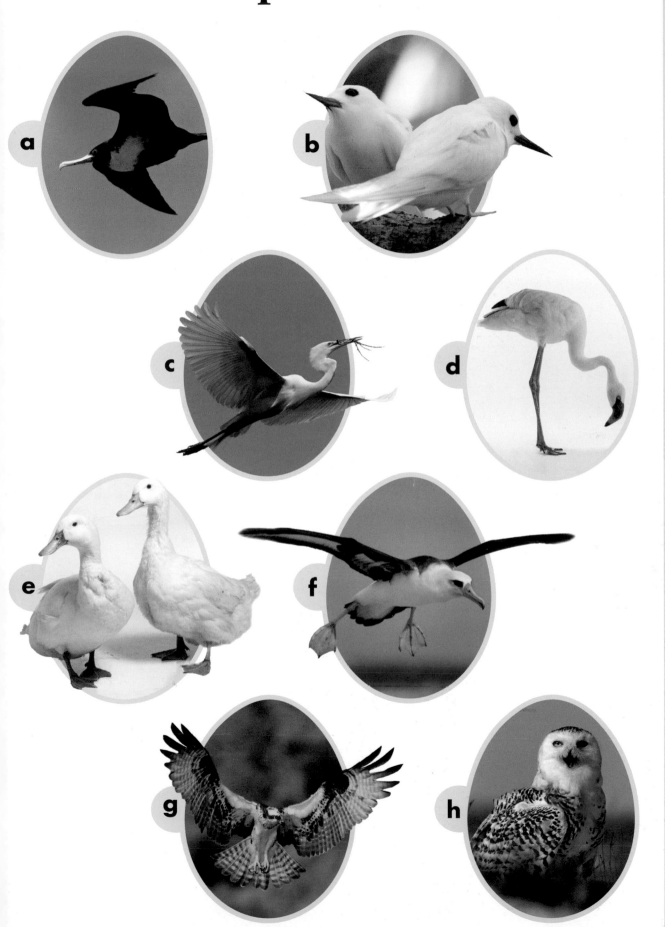

a

b

c

d

e

f

g

h

49

A creche made for 250,000 KINGS

Thousands of penguins packed in tight
Keeping warm through day and night
Fluffy brown chicks huddle together
Safe and dry whatever the weather.

A CLOSER LOOK >

Why the crowds?

These King Penguins live on Antarctic islands where temperatures can fall to **–10°C (14°F).** A lone chick could **freeze**, even with its coating of downy feathers. But a huddle of **hundreds of thousands of penguins** offers protection against the extreme cold.

Are you my daddy?
I thought I was an only child!

I'm hungry!
Where's my fish?

51

Sponge

A hummingbird drinks half its body weight in nectar every day. Its long, brush-tipped tongue has grooves in which the sugary liquid gets collected, in the same way water is absorbed by a sponge.

Chopsticks

Many seabirds have long, narrow bills that they use to probe for food buried in coastal mud. With their extraordinarily long, curved bills, curlews can reach lugworms that hide 1 m (3 ft) deep in thick mud.

Scissors

Birds of prey use their bills not as weapons, but as cutlery. They kill with their talons, and use their bill only to tear and eat flesh. The strong, hooked bill is as efficient at cutting up food as a pair of scissors.

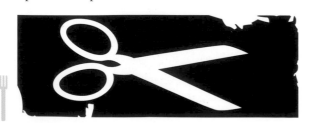

Dagger

A heron goes fishing without a rod or net – a dagger-like bill is all it needs to catch fish. The bird stabs its prey, spearing it on the end of its bill. Then the heron tosses the fish into the air and catches it in its throat.

You can often tell what a bird eats just by looking at the **shape of its bill**. Each bill type acts like a **specialist tool**, perfectly evolved for eating a particular food.

Nutcracker

Short, sharp, and strong, a parrot's bill is the perfect tool for cracking through hard-shelled nuts and seeds. The shells are cracked at the tip of the bill, which is strong and powerful because the bill is short.

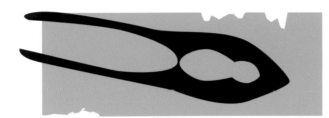

Tweezers

Insect-eating birds such as warblers need precision tools to pick up tiny wriggling bugs among bark and leaves. The slender bill not only fits into narrow crevices, it's also able to hold on to the smallest tidbits.

Tongs

Hornbills find that a long reach is useful when foraging for food. The Red-billed Hornbill is omnivorous – it eats anything, including the eggs of other birds. The bill is hollow and light, so the bird isn't weighed down.

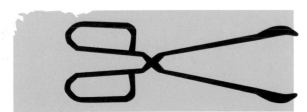

Sieve

Flamingos feed on algae – tiny life forms that live in water. They're too small to be fished out of the water, so instead the bird holds its head upside-down in the water and uses its sieve-like bill to filter out the algae.

How did **this man** discover the mystery of **EVOLUTION?**

CHARLES DARWIN

Charles Darwin was a NATURALIST who, in 1831, set off on a five-year voyage **around the world** in a ship called the *Beagle*. Everywhere it stopped, Darwin collected specimens of animals and plants. One of the places he visited was a cluster of islands off the coast of South America – the *Galápagos Islands*. Among the specimens he found there were several bird species that are found **nowhere else on Earth.**

When Darwin got home, he sent a number of specimens to a specialist for identification. The expert told him that the species were all finches. They had slightly different beaks and body sizes, but they all bore a resemblance to species found in South America. This set Darwin thinking – maybe they had a common ancestor from the mainland.

SOUTH AMERICA

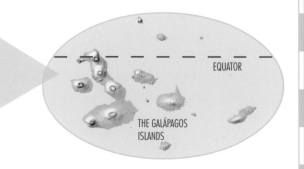

EQUATOR

THE GALÁPAGOS ISLANDS

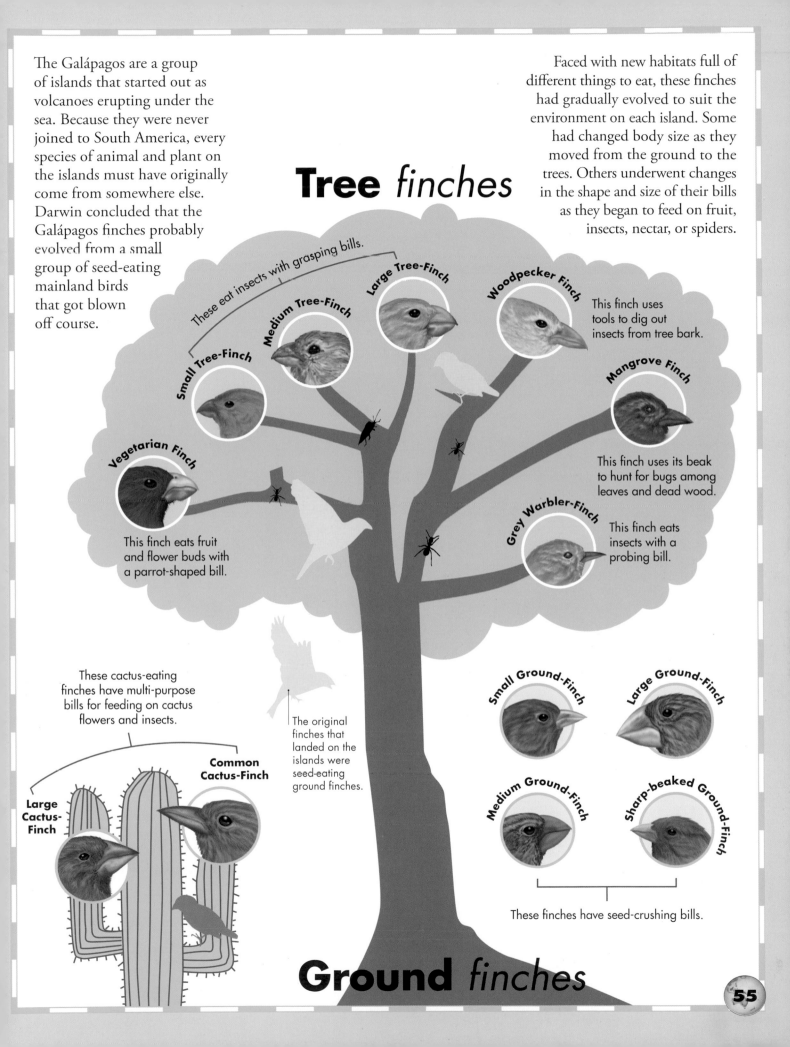

The Galápagos are a group of islands that started out as volcanoes erupting under the sea. Because they were never joined to South America, every species of animal and plant on the islands must have originally come from somewhere else. Darwin concluded that the Galápagos finches probably evolved from a small group of seed-eating mainland birds that got blown off course.

Faced with new habitats full of different things to eat, these finches had gradually evolved to suit the environment on each island. Some had changed body size as they moved from the ground to the trees. Others underwent changes in the shape and size of their bills as they began to feed on fruit, insects, nectar, or spiders.

Tree finches

These eat insects with grasping bills.

Small Tree-Finch

Medium Tree-Finch

Large Tree-Finch

Woodpecker Finch

This finch uses tools to dig out insects from tree bark.

Mangrove Finch

This finch uses its beak to hunt for bugs among leaves and dead wood.

Grey Warbler-Finch

This finch eats insects with a probing bill.

Vegetarian Finch

This finch eats fruit and flower buds with a parrot-shaped bill.

These cactus-eating finches have multi-purpose bills for feeding on cactus flowers and insects.

Common Cactus-Finch

Large Cactus-Finch

The original finches that landed on the islands were seed-eating ground finches.

Small Ground-Finch

Large Ground-Finch

Medium Ground-Finch

Sharp-beaked Ground-Finch

These finches have seed-crushing bills.

Ground finches

How much food?

A lot to swallow

Birds have high-energy lifestyles, so they need a lot of food. Barn Swallows are meat eaters that get protein from their insect-rich diet. It takes a lot of flies and bugs to provide enough protein to help chicks grow.

All in 1 day!

Barn Swallow parents bring food to their chicks 400 times a day!

Why don't birds get fat?
The amount of food a bird eats must be enough to fuel its flight, but not so much that it can't take off.

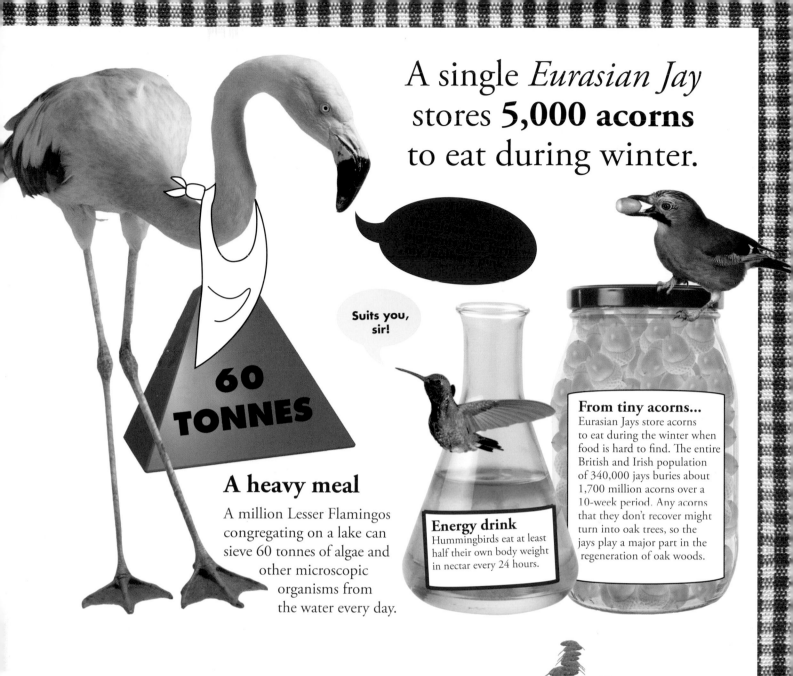

A single *Eurasian Jay* stores **5,000 acorns** to eat during winter.

Suits you, sir!

A heavy meal

A million Lesser Flamingos congregating on a lake can sieve 60 tonnes of algae and other microscopic organisms from the water every day.

60 TONNES

Energy drink
Hummingbirds eat at least half their own body weight in nectar every 24 hours.

From tiny acorns...
Eurasian Jays store acorns to eat during the winter when food is hard to find. The entire British and Irish population of 340,000 jays buries about 1,700 million acorns over a 10-week period. Any acorns that they don't recover might turn into oak trees, so the jays play a major part in the regeneration of oak woods.

A pair of Barn Owls eats **2,000** rodents in **1 year**.

Farmers' friends

Barn Owls are encouraged to roost on farms in the Middle East because they act as natural pest controllers. They are said to be better than pesticides at protecting crops from rodents.

Feed the birds

Legend has it that feeding birds as a hobby was first started by a German baron in the 1880s. Carry on that fine tradition and watch the birds flock to your garden!

Like most birds, I like to find my own food. But as soon as you put food out for me, I will come to rely on you. **So once you start, don't stop!**

What to feed when

SPRING AND SUMMER
Birds need lots of protein when they approach the breeding season – females can use half their reserves laying eggs. Males are busy defending their territory.

 Black sunflower seeds
 Seed mix (no whole peanuts)*

 Juicy (not dry) raisins
 Soft apple or pear cut in half

 Grated mild cheese
 Earthworms

 Mealworms*
 Caterpillars

 Waxworms*
 Dog or cat food (tinned wet food only)

 Dried insect mix*
 Berries

AUTUMN AND WINTER
Natural foods, such as berries, seeds, and insects, can be hard to find in winter. Fatty foods helps birds survive the long, cold, winter nights.

 Bird cake or seed bar
 Seed mix (no whole peanuts)*

 Fat ball
 Soft apple or pear cut in half

 Suet or lard
 Bacon rind

 Stale cake or biscuits
 Cooked rice, pasta, potatoes or pastry

 Wholemeal bread soaked in water
 Grated mild cheese

 Dried insect mix*

* You can buy these from pet shops, garden centres, or online

What's for breakfast?
Seeds and breakfast cereals make ideal bird food. Putting food out early in the morning helps birds recover from cold nights.

Nut warning
Birds like peanuts but they could choke on whole nuts. Put raw, unsalted nuts in a feeder so the birds can peck at them.

Don't put out dry, salty, or spicy foods as these make birds lose a lot of water. Too much dry bread or white bread has the same bad effect.

Birds need plenty of water for drinking, and for bathing! Make sure there's no ice on the water in winter.

Let's make seed cake

You will need:
Mixed bird seed (from a pet store or a bird charity) • Juicy raisins • Grated mild cheese • Suet or lard, at room temperature (but not melted) • Yoghurt pots • String • Thin sticks • Mixing bowl

1. Cut the lard or suet into small pieces. Put in the mixing bowl. Add the other ingredients and mix it up. You can also try adding chopped peanuts, stale cake crumbs, or wholemeal bread.

2. Get stuffing! Pack the mixture into yoghurt pots. Chill it in the fridge for an hour. When it is set, take it out of the pot.

3. Push a stick through the middle of the cake to make a hole. Pass the string through the hole and tie one end around the middle of the stick to make a perch. Use the other end of the string to hang the cake from a tree or fence.

Secret squirrel
It's not just birds that like to be fed. Squirrels will grab every chance of a tree meal, at the expense of the birds.

Birds go nuts for nuts!
Make sure coconuts are fresh, not dried (this can swell up in the bird's stomach and kill it). Reuse old shells by stuffing them with seed cake or suet.

Birds don't need to eat from a table!
You can scatter food on the ground, hang feeders on trees or fences, smear peanut butter on branches, and stuff suet or nuts into holes in trees.

Warning bells
A busy bird table will attract predators. If you have a cat, fix a bell to its collar so the birds can hear it coming and fly away.

59

Chicken facts

Q: Which came first – the chicken or the egg?

A: Biologically speaking, **it was the egg.** Birds evolved from *reptiles*, which evolved from *amphibians* that began to lay their eggs on land.

Chickens are descendants of the Red Junglefowl, which lives in Southeast Asia.

Alektorophobia is the fear of... ... chickens!

Occasionally chickens lay eggs that have no shell. They are known as wind eggs, and are regarded as bad luck in some countries.

Americans eat 8,000,000,000

The domesticated chicken is the most common bird in the world. It is believed that there are more than **24 billion** of them.

You can tell what colour eggs a chicken will lay by looking at its earlobes. White-lobed chickens lay white eggs. A hen with red or dark-coloured lobes will generally lay brown eggs. The exception is the Araucana.

The most yolks ever found in a single egg is **nine**.

Only cockerels (male chickens) make crowing noises.

There are about **5 billion** egg-laying hens in the world, each producing around 300 eggs a year.

Combover

Chickens have one of eight different styles of comb – the buttercup, the cushion, the pea, the rose, the silkie, the strawberry, the V-shaped, and the single. Chickens can get frostbite on their comb if the temperature drops too low.

The droppings produced by a chicken in its lifetime produce enough energy to power a 100 W light bulb for 5 hours.

Chickens have wings but rarely fly farther than the nearest tree. The longest recorded flight for a chicken is 13 seconds.

chickens a year.

When chickens go wild

Colonies of feral chickens have set up home in several places in America, including the Hollywood freeway, Miami, and Hawaii. Every now and then, they have to be rounded up to keep their numbers down, but there are always some that get away.

The Araucana or Americana (or even Ameraucana) chicken lays blue or green eggs. It is also known as the "Easter Egg" chicken.

WELCOME TO CHICKEN

A town in Alaska was named "Chicken" because nobody could agree how to spell the name of the bird they wanted to name it after – the ptarmigan. (Well, it's a bit like a chicken.)

That's a whopping
1.5 trillion eggs every year!

WORKING BIRDS

Hunting with eagles has been part of Kazakh culture for 6,000 years. A Golden Eagle appears on the Kazakh flag, and a traditional proverb says, "Fine horses and fierce eagles are the wings of Kazakhs." For the *berkutchi*, or hunter, using birds for hunting is more than a sport – it is a way of life. He learns the same skills that have been passed from father to son for generations – how to capture and train the fierce bird that will hunt foxes for him every winter for the next 10 years.

HANDLE WITH CARE
A *berkutchi* treats his eagle well. As a chick, it is fed by hand so that it gets used to humans. The bird then knows who's boss and will come quickly when called.

Female Golden Eagles are the ideal hunting bird.
Larger and stronger than the males, these birds can grow to 90 cm (3 ft) from head to tail, with a wingspan of 2.3 m (7½ ft). They can kill a fox with a single strike of their talons.

TRAINING

The eagle is tamed for a month and trained over the summer. Part of its training is knowing not to attack its owner's flocks.

WHICH CHICK?

A *berkutchi* may catch 10 to 15 chicks before finding the right one to train. Those less than seven years old make the best hunters.

THE HUNT

The eagle is made to wear a hood so it is not distracted, and ridden out to the grassland. The hood is removed, the bird flies off...

ESSENTIAL EQUIPMENT

A cowhide glove protects the *berkutchi* against the eagle's sharp talons. He grips its tethers firmly to stop it flying away.

SUCCESS

... and the kill is made. The *berkutchi* lures the eagle away from its prey (a fox) with food. The fox is left intact, its fur to be used for hats and clothes in the freezing Kazakh winter.

Each eagle is kept for a maximum of 10 hunting seasons.
Then it is returned to the wild. The Kazakhs take care not to harm eagle populations, although other traders are greedy and catch large numbers of birds of prey for sale.

DIVING BIRDS

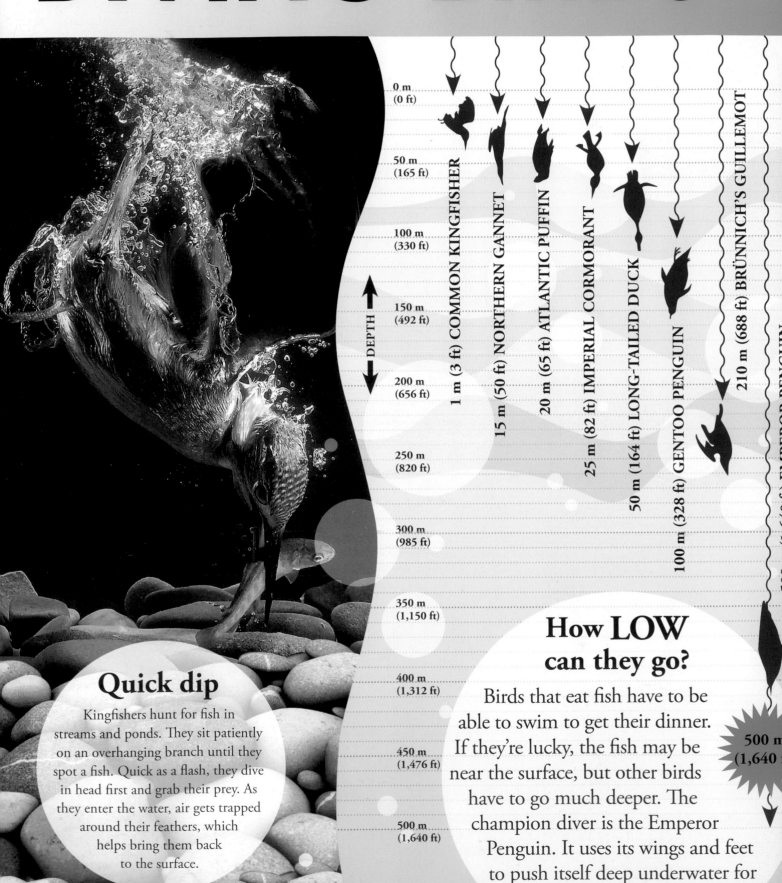

Depth	
0 m (0 ft)	
50 m (165 ft)	
100 m (330 ft)	
150 m (492 ft)	
200 m (656 ft)	
250 m (820 ft)	
300 m (985 ft)	
350 m (1,150 ft)	
400 m (1,312 ft)	
450 m (1,476 ft)	
500 m (1,640 ft)	

1 m (3 ft) COMMON KINGFISHER

15 m (50 ft) NORTHERN GANNET

20 m (65 ft) ATLANTIC PUFFIN

25 m (82 ft) IMPERIAL CORMORANT

50 m (164 ft) LONG-TAILED DUCK

100 m (328 ft) GENTOO PENGUIN

210 m (688 ft) BRÜNNICH'S GUILLEMOT

500 m (1,640 ft) EMPEROR PENGUIN

Quick dip

Kingfishers hunt for fish in streams and ponds. They sit patiently on an overhanging branch until they spot a fish. Quick as a flash, they dive in head first and grab their prey. As they enter the water, air gets trapped around their feathers, which helps bring them back to the surface.

How LOW can they go?

Birds that eat fish have to be able to swim to get their dinner. If they're lucky, the fish may be near the surface, but other birds have to go much deeper. The champion diver is the Emperor Penguin. It uses its wings and feet to push itself deep underwater for up to 10 minutes at a time.

500 m (1,640 ft)

DIVE, DIVE, DIVE!

Plunge divers, such as gannets, boobies, and brown pelicans, catch fast-moving fish by diving from high up in the sky. The speed at which they enter the water overcomes their natural buoyancy and helps them go deep below the surface. As they enter the water they fold their wings back to make a streamlined shape that prevents them hurting themselves.

In pursuit

Birds that swim after their prey are called pursuit divers. They propel themselves using their wings (penguins, auks, and petrels) or feet (grebes, divers, and cormorants). Although it takes energy to swim, they catch more fish than seabirds that just put their heads under the water.

What are you talking about?

The language of birds is among the most complex of any animal. They have a variety of calls and songs – but what exactly are they trying to say?

Call or song?

Birds make two main types of sound – calls and songs. Calls are short and simple, but songs can be long and complicated. Songs are used to announce ownership of a territory and to attract a mate. Usually, it is the male that sings his heart out during the breeding season. However, in some species the female sings along too, and the pair perform a duet together.

Where is the syrinx?

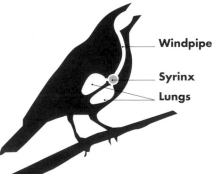

Windpipe
Syrinx
Lungs

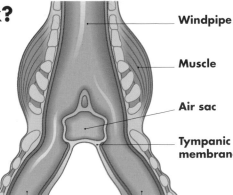

Windpipe
Muscle
Air sac
Tympanic membrane
Towards lungs

THE SYRINX
Birds have a unique sound-producing organ called the syrinx, not found in any other animal. It is located in their chest. As air flows out from the lungs, it passes through the syrinx, which causes a system of membranes to vibrate, producing sound. Muscles stretch or squeeze the membranes to give precise control of pitch and loudness.

DANGER!

One sound that every bird knows from a young age is the alarm call. This means there's danger present – a predator, such as a hawk or fox. Some birds have different alarms that call for different actions from their flock or chicks – to be silent and hide, to flee, or to attack the intruder. When a female duck raises the alarm, her ducklings immediately dive and swim underwater to safety.

GO AWAY!

Birds use aggression calls to protect their territory, mates, or sources of food. If one bird gets too close to another, the two will start to have a bit of a shouting match. The calls are often accompanied with defensive actions, such as squaring up to each other or chasing one another away.

WHERE ARE YOU?

In a dense habitat, such as a forest, birds can't always see each other. So they use calls to keep in touch. As the members of a flock spread out to feed, they call constantly to each other. In a crowded colony, birds call to locate their partners and chicks. An adult Emperor Penguin can recognize the voice of its mate and chick among the din of hundreds of other penguins in the colony. Even more impressively, it can remember these unique calls despite having been away, sometimes for weeks at a time.

CHICK CHAT

Birds begin to make calls at an early age – a nest full of chicks is a noisy place as they all beg for food. In some species, calling starts even before hatching. Quail chicks call to each other and to their mother from inside their eggs. By listening to their parents while still in the egg, developing chicks can recognize them even before hatching. Stone-curlew chicks are able to run as soon as they hatch, so recognizing their parents' calls will help to stop them straying too far.

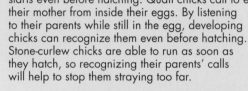

MATE WITH ME!

The main reason birds sing is to attract mates during courtship. However, there are other ways to produce an attention-grabbing song than just singing. Woodpigeons clap their wing tips together, making a loud whip-crack sound. Flappet Larks beat their wings rapidly, making a loud thrumming noise as they climb into the sky. A male Princess Stephanie bird of paradise makes a loud rustling noise with his wings and tail, and woodpeckers hammer their bills against trees or poles. Storks clash their bills together in a kind of greeting – but as they have no syrinx, they are mute and can't make any calls at all.

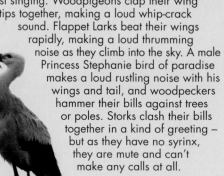

Big-brained BIRDS

Calling someone a birdbrain is supposed to be an insult, but today we know that some birds are actually pretty intelligent. So who's got the brightest brain in the bird world?

Why did the crow cross the road?

In some Japanese towns, Carrion Crows like to hang around at traffic lights – not to cross the road, but to crack nuts! When the traffic stops at a red light, a crow drops a nut in the middle of the road. At the green light, the traffic drives over the nut, crushing the shell. When the lights turn back to red, the crow hops down and pecks up the tasty kernel inside.

Relative to body size, a crow's brain is the same size as a chimp's brain. That's HUGE.

Yeah. A bird's eyes are usually bigger than its brain. Did you just see a car...?

Many crows pass the intelligence test, but they're not the only brainboxes in birdland...

Tooled up

Woodpecker Finches use cactus needles to probe for grubs in tree trunks, but New Caledonian Crows (named after their home island in the Pacific) can make their own tools. Using their bills as scissors, they trim twigs into hooks and shred leaves into brushes to help them catch insects. Captive crows have been known to bend wire into hooks.

Right, found number 18,468. Now where did I stash 18,469?

Memory masters

A Clark's Nutcracker (a type of small crow) may bury a food store of more than 30,000 pine seeds in autumn. Amazingly, it remembers where they are and can retrieve them up to eight months later, even if the seeds have since been covered in leaves or snow. Jays – members of the crow family – can find acorns a year after burying them.

Fisher kings

Some heron species catch fish by dropping bait, such as bread, insects, worms, twigs, and feathers, into the water. Black Herons also make an umbrella-like shade with their wings over the water's surface, blocking out reflections so they can see the fish beneath.

I'm off!

Who's a clever boy, then? Oh, I am!

Pretty clever Polly

Parrots are known to be intelligent birds and can copy human speech. One captive African Grey Parrot, called Alex, went one better – he could not only imitate sounds but actually talk. He was taught to count, say "yes" and "no", and say the name and colour of more than 100 items, such as wool or food, when he was shown them.

The King Vulture has a wingspan of 2 m (6½ ft), making it one of the largest American vultures.

The clean-up crew

Egyptian Vulture

Vultures are large birds with a broad wingspan that they use for soaring high in the sky on thermals. They have an unfairly sinister reputation – especially when seen circling the sky or sitting with their necks hunched, waiting for an injured animal to die. However, vultures have an important part to play in an ecosystem. These scavenging birds help to break up a carcass so that other organisms can get in to feed on it.

King Vulture

Turkey vulture

African vultures rely on their excellent eyesight to find carcasses, while most American vultures use smell. The majority of species have no feathers on their face, and sometimes their necks, which makes it easier to stay clean when eating a messy carcass. The bill is hooked for ripping through skin and fur – even tough mammal hide is no problem for most vulture species.

The King Vulture has one of the most spectacular faces in the bird world. As well as the brightly coloured skin on its head, neck, and earlobes, it has a fleshy orange growth above its bill, called a caruncle. The size of the caruncle determines who gets the first peck at a carcass. Although it usually follows other types of vulture when searching for food, once it lands, other scavengers get out of its way. That's why it's the king of all the vultures.

White-backed Vulture

Although vultures are classed as birds of prey, they rarely attack a healthy animal. Instead, they wait for another predator to make a kill or they find an already dead animal. They eat as much as they can, then find somewhere to sit and digest it. A vulture's stomach acid is so strong it can kill bacteria that would make other animals sick.

White-backed Vultures feeding

Back OFF!

Birds can get aggressive over territory, mates, and food, and it's not always easy to escape if your attacker is bigger or faster than you. But some birds have other methods of defence...

Spit it out

Fulmar chicks are often preyed on by birds of prey and large gulls, but they can strike back with foul-smelling vomit that contains acid and fish oil. The chicks can fire their vomit 1.5 m (5 ft). The attacker steers well clear of the vomit as it can ruin the waterproofing on its feathers.

Blending in

A frogmouth's first line of defence is camouflage, as it looks not unlike a branch when it stands still. If that doesn't work, the element of surprise just might: the bird will flash open its bright yellow eyes and huge mouth, startling the predator just long enough for it to make an escape.

Not dead, merely resting

Plovers lead predators away from their eggs by pretending to be injured. An injured bird is easy prey, so the predator is attracted to the plover, which crawls away from the nest. When the predator has followed far enough, the plover recovers and flies away, safe.

Oh, my poor wing!

Final warning

Many birds adopt threat displays, such as a wide open bill, raised crest feathers, or ruffled wings. A threatened Sunbittern suddenly flicks its wings wide open to reveal huge spots that look like staring eyes. The sight of these giant "eyeballs" sends most intruders packing.

Strength in numbers

It's much harder for a predator to focus on a single bird among many, especially when there are so many pairs of eyes on the lookout. And if the odd member of a flock is taken, at least there's the rest of the flock to ensure the survival of the species.

The power of poo

Fulmars may have toxic vomit, but Fieldfares prefer to use the other end to squirt out their defensive liquid. A flock of Fieldfares can deliver huge amounts of excrement with great accuracy, so that their attacker is left dripping in droppings.

Kicking back

Cassowaries are huge flightless birds that seem pretty scary from their size alone, but they also carry offensive weapons – a huge claw on their middle toe. They have been known to kill a man by jumping up and slashing him across the stomach.

RECORD BREAKERS

SURVIVOR In 1945, a chicken hit back against the axe – and won! Nicknamed Mike, the "headless" chicken (which still had its brain stem and jugular vein intact) lived for another 18 months. Its owner fed him with an eyedropper, dripping grain and water down the chicken's open neck.

smallest widest fastest longest biggest

Fastest
FLIGHT

When diving to catch prey, the **Peregrine Falcon** can accelerate up to 200 kph (124 mph). This makes it the record holder for fastest freefall flight, but the fastest level flight is 169 kph (105 mph), achieved by the White-throated Needletail (a swift). The fastest birds in the water are Gentoo Penguins, reaching 30 kph (19 mph).

Most
FEATHERS

Flying farther north than any other swan species, the **Tundra Swan** has the highest number of feathers of any bird during winter. Its 25,000 feather count keeps it warm as it nests within the Arctic Circle.

Widest
WINGSPAN

The Wandering Albatross has a spectacular wingspan of 3 m (10 ft) – the widest of any bird – for soaring over the ocean.

Biggest BILL

Male Australian Pelicans have the biggest bills of any bird. The largest measured was 43 cm (17 in) long. The Sword-billed Hummingbird has the longest bill in relation to its body length – the bill, measuring 10 cm (4 in), is longer than its body.

Smallest BIRD

A male Bee Hummingbird is as small as your thumb – around 5 cm (2 in) long. Half of that is made up of its bill and tail. This same species builds one of the smallest nests, around the size of an eggcup.

A single ostrich egg weighs the same as about 20 chicken eggs. It takes 2 hours to hard boil – but makes a big omelette!

HUNGRIEST **A male Emperor Penguin** is a devoted father. In the breeding season, he incubates the egg and then looks after the chick, often enduring Antarctic blizzards. During this time – which can last up to 4 months – he doesn't eat a thing and can lose nearly half of his body weight.

ACTUAL SIZE

You could fit around 2,000 Vervain Hummingbird eggs inside one ostrich egg.

smallest widest fastest

Champion
WEIGHTLIFTER

A North American **Bald Eagle** has been reported to have taken off with a mule deer fawn weighing 6.8 kg (15 lb) in its talons. It was once claimed that a **White-tailed Sea Eagle** carried a four-year-old girl for 1.6 km (1 mile) before dropping her unharmed.

Biggest
NEST

Malleefowl build mounds that can be 4.5 m (15 ft) high and 10.5 m (34 ft) wide. The nest is made of around 300 tonnes of rotting vegetation and stinks like a compost heap, but it keeps the eggs safe and warm.

Heaviest
FLYING BIRD

The male **Kori Bustard** weighs up to 19 kg (42 lb). It's quite an achievement that it ever gets off the ground.

MOST NUMEROUS
Wild bird

Red-billed Queleas are the most numerous wild birds on the planet. These African birds congregate in huge flocks of hundreds of thousands of birds, which can take hours to fly past the same spot.

Ostriches have the biggest eyes of any land animal, around 5 cm (2 in) across.

Big BIRD

The tallest bird ever recorded was an **ostrich** that measured 2.74 m (9 ft) tall. Ostriches also, unsurprisingly, lay the biggest eggs, averaging 15 to 20 cm (6 to 8 in) in diameter, and weighing around 1.5 kg. (3.5 lb). (The record for the largest egg in relation to body size belongs to the kiwi – it lays a whopper one quarter of its own body weight. Ouch!) A further record set by the ostrich is the land-speed record for birds; it can run at 72 kph (45 mph).

Smallest EGG

Vervain Hummingbirds lay the smallest eggs, which is just as well considering they build nests the size of half a walnut. Their eggs are just 1 cm (2/5 in) long.

FASTEST flapper

All hummingbirds – which are the only birds that can fly upside-down and backwards – are fast flappers. However, the fastest is a South American species of hummingbird called the **Horned Sungem**, which beats its wings 90 times a second. That takes a lot of energy, which explains why hummingbirds are also the biggest eaters of the bird world, consuming half their body weight in nectar and insects every day.

HIGHEST flier

Rüppell's Vultures circle the thermals above all other birds. The highest recorded flight was at 11,277 m (37,000 ft) above sea level.

The vulture's record-breaking height was known because it collided with an aircraft flying over Africa.

LONGEST MIGRATION

The Arctic Tern flies the longest migration route of any bird, covering a distance of up to 20,000 km (12,500 miles) each way from the Arctic Circle to Antarctica. But the longest trip on record was made by a Sooty Shearwater (a kind of seabird), which was fitted with a satellite transmitter at its nest in New Zealand in 2005. It flew 64,037 km (39,800 miles) across the Pacific Ocean in 262 days.

WORKING WITH BIRDS

*Some birds are used
to scare other birds.*

*Eat up if you want to be
a big healthy grown-up.*

BIRD CONTROL

Hitting a flock of birds could endanger an aeroplane, so predatory birds, such as falcons, are sometimes used on airfields to frighten the flock off.

Bird controllers are vital at airports, where they prevent large flocks of birds from landing on the runway. Their job is to monitor the airfield and scare any birds away just before aeroplanes take off and land. If a bird gets sucked into an engine it could cause a plane to crash.

AVICULTURALIST

Breeding rare birds in captivity is one way of ensuring that species that are threatened in the wild do not die out.

Aviculturalists breed and keep wild birds. Usually this is to preserve a species that is rare or under threat in its natural environment. Sometimes the birds are released back into the wild. Aviculturalists often do this as a hobby, focusing on particular species or groups of birds, or as part of a research or conservation team.

*August is not a good time
to be a gamebird.*

*Learning about birds
helps us to preserve them.*

GAMEKEEPER

Shooting grouse and other game birds is a key industry in the countryside. Birds are raised specifically for this purpose.

Gamekeepers raise birds on a country estate for shoots. The gamekeeper breeds the birds from eggs and protects and cares for them as they grow. Part of the job involves maintaining the right environment for the birds, which may require burning or cutting back undergrowth. Controlling predators is an important part of the job.

ORNITHOLOGIST

Learning about how birds live is an important part of an ornithologist's job. Very little is known about some of the rarest species.

An ornithologist is a scientist who specializes in birds. Ornithologists investigate bird behaviour, lifestyles, anatomy, feeding, breeding, distribution, migration, and habitats. Often they focus on one particular type of bird or certain types of bird behaviour.

*Who are you calling
an ugly duckling?*

*They're a bit fiddly
to get out of a net.*

POULTRY FARMER

Chicken is the world's favourite meat, so farmers have to raise large flocks of these birds to make sure there are enough drumsticks to go around.

Some farmers raise birds for their eggs or for their meat. Egg farmers mainly keep chickens, though some specialize in duck or quail eggs. Others raise eggs of gamebirds, which they provide as chicks to gamekeepers. Farmers who keep poultry for meat breed all sorts of birds – mainly chickens, though sometimes even ostriches.

VOLUNTEERS

Carrying out bird surveys can involve trapping birds in nets to check weights and health before releasing them back into the wild.

Volunteers are usually members of a bird society or charity. Their activities include carrying out surveys of bird numbers, guarding nests of protected birds, rescuing injured birds, caring for them at sanctuaries, and washing birds oiled in a tanker spill.

We've got this one's number.

*This won't hurt –
believe me, I'm a vet.*

BIRD BANDER

Each banded bird has a unique number that enables researchers to find out where it was banded and where it has been.

These researchers mainly study migration through banding and tracking birds. They capture birds safely and check their condition and sex, before placing a numbered band around the bird's leg. Any bird found with a band can then be traced. Sometimes birds are fitted with a tracking device that allows scientists to follow birds without having to catch them.

AVIAN VET

Looking after the birds at a poultry farm requires the attention of a specialized vet to make sure the flock stays healthy.

Avian vets specialize in birds, which is often regarded as a separate branch of veterinary medicine. Most vets can deal with the common complaints of domestic birds, such as budgies, but unusual species, wild birds, and poultry often need the attention of someone who has more experience in that field.

GLOSSARY

altitude Height of an object, animal, or place above sea level

alula Small group of between two and six feathers that covers a bird's "thumb". The alula can be raised to reduce turbulence during flight

avian Things of or relating to birds. For example, avian flu is a type of flu spread by birds

barb Small branch that sticks out from a feather's central shaft. Each feather has thousands of barbs, creating a smooth surface

barbules Every barb on a feather has many tiny side branches called barbules. These hook onto other barbules like a zip or Velcro

bill Jaws of a bird. A bill is also known as a beak

bower Showground built by a male bowerbird to attract a mate

colony Large group of animals living close together. Birds often gather in colonies during the breeding season

creche Group of young birds of about the same age, produced by different parents

crop Part of the digestive system in birds, which stores food after it has been swallowed

down feather Soft, fluffy feather that provides good insulation

endangered species Rare species at risk of extinction

extinction Point at which no living members of a species exists

gizzard Bag-like structure that forms part of a bird's stomach, where tough food is ground up. Seed-eating birds have large gizzards

incubating When a parent bird sits on its eggs to keep them warm so that they can develop and hatch

keel Long, broad ridge on a bird's breastbone to which the wing muscles are attached

migration Long journey by an animal to find a new place to live. Many birds migrate regularly every year

passerine Bird with feet that are adapted for perching on branches and twigs

plumage All of a bird's feathers

predator Animal that kills and eats other animals

prey Animal that is killed and eaten by a predator

scavenger Animal that feeds on the remains of dead animals

syrinx Sound-making organ inside a bird's windpipe. It enables birds to produce calls and songs

talons Sharp claws of a meat-eating bird such as an eagle, falcon, or owl

thermal Column of rising warm air. Some birds, such as vultures and eagles, hitch a lift on thermals to soar high in the sky

wingspan Distance across a bird's back and outstretched wings. It is measured from one wingtip to another

Laughing Kookaburra growing up

Hatching

Three hours old

Seven days old

18 days old

INDEX

22 days old   31 days old   60 days old

CREDITS

Dorling Kindersley would like to thank the following people for their help with this book: Leon Gray, Elinor Greenwood, and Ben Morgan for additional editing; Claire Patane for additional design; Simon Mumford for cartography; Emma Shepherd, Lucy Claxton, Myriam Megharbi, Karen VanRoss, and Romaine Werblow in the DK Picture Library.

Dorling Kindersley would also like to thank the following for their kind permission to reproduce their photographs:
(Key: a-above; b-below/bottom; c-centre; f-far; l-left; r-right; t-top)